Poems about Animals
What Fun to be a Hippo

Chosen by Wendy Cooling

Illustrated by Anthony Lewis

First published in 2000 by Franklin Watts
96, Leonard Street, London EC2A 4XD

Franklin Watts Australia
14 Mars Road, Lane Cove, NSW 2066

© in this anthology Wendy Cooling 2000
Illustration © Anthony Lewis 2000

Editor: Sarah Snashall
Designer: Louise Thomas
Border artwork: Diana Mayo

ISBN   0 7496 3478 2 (Hbk)
        0 7496 3840 0 (Big Book)
        0 7496 3912 1 (Pbk)

Dewey classification 821.008

Printed in Hong Kong/China

Acknowledgments

The editor and publishers gratefully acknowledge permission to reproduce the following copyright material.

Wasps, by Dorothy Aldis, from *Is Anybody Hungry?* by Dorothy Aldis. © Dorothy Aldis. Used by permission of G. P. Puttnam & Sons, a division of Penguin Puttnam Inc. *Bees*, by Jack Prelutsky. From *Zoo Doings*, 1979. Reprinted with permission of Greenwillow Books, a division of William Morrow & Co. *A Dragon Fly*, by Eleanor Farjeon, from *Silver, Sand and Snow* (Michael Joseph). Reprinted by permission of the author, c/o David Higham Associates, 5-8 Lower John Street, Golden Square, London W1R 4HA. *I Feel Sorry for the Slug*, by Judith Nicholls. © Judith Nicholls. Reprinted by permission of the author. *Riddle*, by Judith Nicholls. © Judith Nicholls 1990. First published in *Higgledy-Humbug*, by Judith Nicholls, published by Mary Glasgow Publications. Reprinted by permission of the author. *Mice*, by Rose Fyleman. Permission granted by The Society of Authors as the literary representative of the Estate of Rose Fyleman. *The Sparrow*, by Aileen Fisher, from *Feathered Ones and Furry*, by Aileen Fisher. © 1971, 1999 Aileen Fisher. Used by permission of Marian Reiner for the author. *The Squirrel*, by Ted Hughes. Reprinted by permission of Faber and Faber Ltd. *Dogs*, by Marchette Chute. © 1957 by E. P. Dutton. Copyright renewed 1985 by Marchette Chute. Reprinted by permission of Elizabeth Hauser. *Don't Call Alligator Long-Mouth till You Cross River*, by John Agard, from *Say It Again, Granny* (The Bodley Head). Reprinted by permission of The Random House Group Ltd. *Zebra Question*, by Shel Silverstein. From *A Light in the Attic*, by Shel Silverstein. © 1981 by Evil Eye Music Inc. Reprinted by permission of Edite Kroll Literary Agency. *Tigers*, by Jean Kenward. Permission granted by the author. *Tall Boy*, by Faustin Charles. From *Once Upon an Animal*, by Faustin Charles (Bloomsbury). Permission granted by the author. *Hippo Writes a Love Poem to his Wife* and *Hippo Writes a Love Poem to her Husband*, by John Agard. By kind permission of John Agard c/o Caroline Sheldon Literary Agency. *Hippo Writes a Love Poem to his Wife* and *Hippo Writes a Love Poem to her Husband* from *We Animals Would Like a Word with You*, published by Random House (1996). *The Hippopotamus*, by Michael Flanders. Reprinted with permission of the Michael Flanders Estate. *Rhinoceros*, by Giles Andreae, from *Rumble in the Jungle*. Reprinted by permission of Orchard Books.

Every effort has been made to trace copyright, but if any omissions have been made please let us know in order that we may put it right in the next edition.

Contents

Ants Although Admirable,
Are Awfully Aggravating

The busy ant works hard all day
And never seems to rest or play.
He carries things ten times his size,
And never grumbles, whines or cries.
And even climbing flower stalks,
He always runs, he never walks.
He loves his work, he never tires,
And never puffs, pants or perspires.

Yet though I praise his boundless vim
I am not really fond of him.

by Walter R. Brooks

The Spider

I'm told that the spider
Has coiled up inside her
Enough silky material
To spin an aerial
One-way track
To the moon and back
Whilst I
Cannot even catch a fly.

Anon

Wasps

Wasps like coffee.
Syrup.
Tea.
Coca-Cola.
Butter.
Me.

by Dorothy Aldis

Bees

Every bee
that
ever was
was
partly
sting
and partly
...buzz.

by Jack Prelutsky

Mumbling Bees

All around the garden flowers
Big velvet bees are bumbling,
They hover low as they go
They're mumbling, mumbling, mumbling.

    To lavender and snapdragons
      The busy bees keep coming,
      And all the busy afternoon
    They're humming, humming, humming.

Inside each bell-shaped flower and rose
They busily go stumbling,
Collecting pollen all day long
And bumbling, bumbling, bumbling.

by Daphne Lister

A Dragonfly

When the heat of the summer
Made drowsy the land,
A dragonfly came
And sat on my hand,
With its blue jointed body,
And wings like spun glass
It lit on my fingers
As though they were grass.

by Eleanor Farjeon

I Feel Sorry for the Slug

He has to live on cabbage –
rather him than me!
I really wouldn't want to eat
just leaves AND leaves for tea.

(and leaves and leaves and leaves and leaves and
leaves...)

by Judith Nicholls

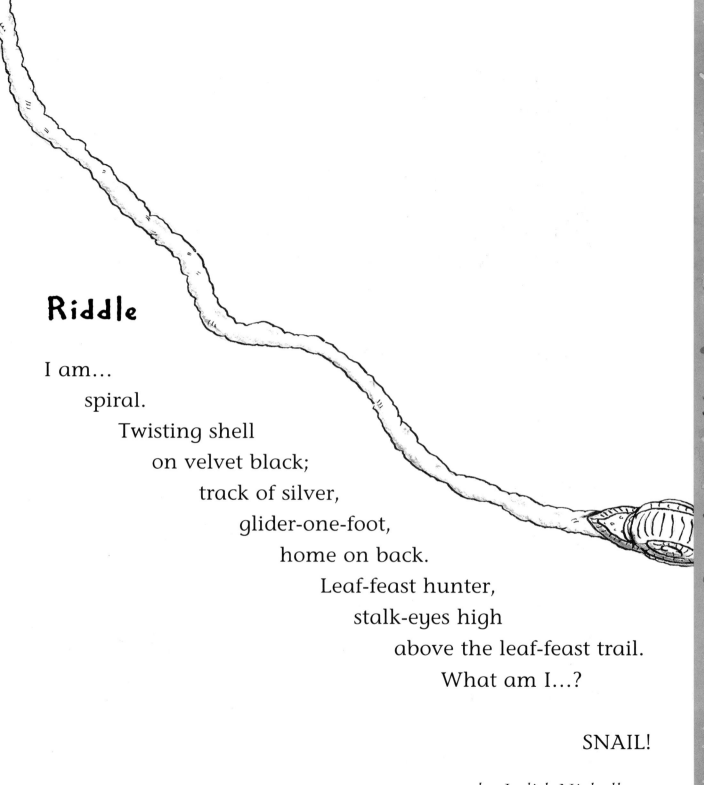

Riddle

I am…
    spiral.
        Twisting shell
           on velvet black;
               track of silver,
                 glider-one-foot,
                   home on back.
                     Leaf-feast hunter,
                       stalk-eyes high
                         above the leaf-feast trail.
                         What am I…?

SNAIL!

by Judith Nicholls

9

Mice

I think mice
Are rather nice.

Their tails are long,
Their faces small,
They haven't any
Chins at all.
Their ears are pink,
Their teeth are white,
They run about
The house at night.
They nibble things
They shouldn't touch
And no one seems
To like them much.

But I think mice
Are nice.

by Rose Fyleman

Frog

A frog once went out walking,
In the pleasant summer air,
He happened into a barber's shop
And skipped into the chair.
The barber said in disbelief:
"Your brains are surely bare.
How can you have a haircut
When you haven't any hair?"

Anon

The Sparrow

I found a speckled sparrow
between the showers of rain.

He thought the window wasn't there
and flew against the pane.

I picked him up and held him.
He didn't stir at all.

I hardly felt him in my hand,
he was so soft and small.

I held him like a flower
upon my open palm.

I saw an eyelid quiver,
though he lay still and calm.

And then...before I knew it
I stood alone, aghast:

I never thought a bird so limp
could fly away so fast!

by Aileen Fisher

The Day of the Gulls

On a silver-cold day
Under snow-heavy clouds
The seagulls come
Driven inland
Swooping and screaming
Over the scraps in the gutters.

The children stare
As the street is made beautiful
By the white shining
Of their wings.

by Jennifer Curry

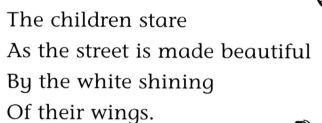

The Eagle

He clasps the crag with crooked hands:
Close to the sun in lonely lands,
Ringed with the azure world, he stands.

The wrinkled sea beneath him crawls;
He watches from his mountain walls,
And like a thunderbolt he falls.

by Alfred Lord Tennyson

13

Whisky Frisky

Whisky Frisky, hippity-hop
Up he goes to the treetop!

Whirly, twirly, round and round,
Down he scampers to the ground.

Furly, curly, what a tail!
Tall as a feather, broad as a sail!

Where's his supper? In the shell.
Snappity, crackity, out it fell.

Anon

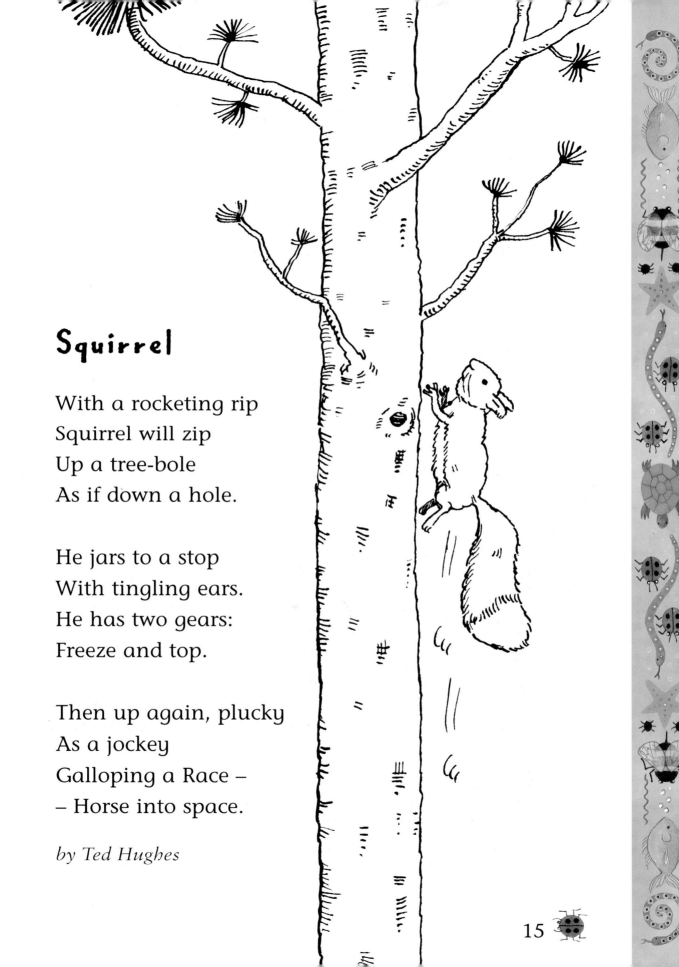

Squirrel

With a rocketing rip
Squirrel will zip
Up a tree-bole
As if down a hole.

He jars to a stop
With tingling ears.
He has two gears:
Freeze and top.

Then up again, plucky
As a jockey
Galloping a Race –
– Horse into space.

by Ted Hughes

15

Alley Cat

A bit of jungle in the street.
He goes on velvet toes
And, slinking through the shadows, stalks
Imaginary foes.

Anon

Choosing Their Names

Our old cat has kittens three –
What do you think their names should be?

One is a tabby, with emerald eyes,
    And a tail that's long and slender,
And into a temper she quickly flies
    If you ever by chance offend her.
      I think we shall call her this –
      I think we shall call her that –
Now, don't you think that Pepperpot
    Is a nice name for a cat?

One is black, with a frill of white,
    And her feet are all white fur, too;
If you stroke her she carries her tail upright
    And quickly begins to purr, too!
        I think we shall call her this –
        I think we shall call her that –
Now don't you think that Sootikin
    Is a nice name for a cat?

One is tortoise-shell, yellow and black,
    With plenty of white about him;
If you tease him, at once he sets up his back:
        He's a quarrelsome one, ne'er doubt him.
        I think we shall call him this –
        I think we shall call him that –
Now don't you think that Scratchaway
    Is a nice name for a cat?

Our old cat has kittens three
And I fancy these their names will be:
Pepperpot, Sootikin, Scratchaway – there!
Were ever kittens with these to compare?
And we call the old mother –
                Now, what do you think?
Tabitha Longclaws Tiddley Wink.

by Thomas Hood

Dogs

The dogs I know
Have many shapes.
For some are big and tall,
And some are long,
And some are thin,
And some are fat and small.
And some are little bits of fluff
And have no shape at all.

by Marchette Chute

I've Got a Dog

I've got a dog as thin as a rail,
He's got fleas all over his tail;
Every time his tail goes flop,
The fleas on the bottom all hop to the top.

Anon

The Donkey

I saw a donkey
One day old,
His head was too big
For his neck to hold;
His legs were shaky
And long and loose,
They rocked and staggered
And weren't much use.

He tried to gambol
And frisk a bit,
But he wasn't quite sure
Of the trick of it.
His queer little coat
Was soft and grey,
And curled at his neck
In a lovely way.

He looked so little
And weak and slim,
I prayed the world
Might be good to him.

Anon

The Kangaroo

Old Jumpety-Bumpety-Hop-and-Go-One
Was lying asleep on his side in the sun.
This old kangaroo, he was whisking the flies
(With his long glossy tail) from his ears and his eyes.
Jumpety-Bumpety-Hop-and-Go-One
Was lying asleep on his side in the sun,
Jumpety-Bumpety-Hop!

Traditional Australian

Crocodile Alphabet

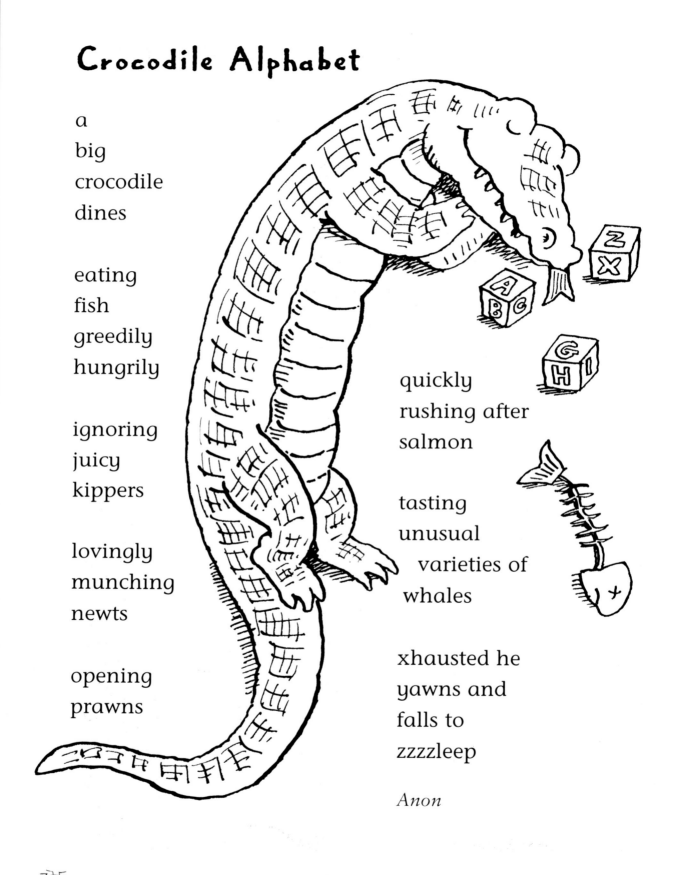

a
big
crocodile
dines

eating
fish
greedily
hungrily

ignoring
juicy
kippers

lovingly
munching
newts

opening
prawns

quickly
rushing after
salmon

tasting
unusual
varieties of
whales

xhausted he
yawns and
falls to
zzzzleep

Anon

Don't Call Alligator Long-Mouth till You Cross River

Call alligator long-mouth
call alligator saw-mouth
call alligator pushy-mouth
call alligator scissors-mouth
call alligator raggedy-mouth
call alligator bumpy-bum
call alligator all dem rude word
but better wait

till you cross river.

by John Agard

23

Zebra Question

I asked the zebra,
Are you black with white stripes?
Or white with black stripes?
And the zebra asked me,
Are you good with bad habits?
Or are you bad with good habits?
Are you noisy with quiet times?
Or are you quiet with noisy times?
Are you happy with some sad days?
Or are you sad with some happy days?
Are you neat with some sloppy ways?
Or are you sloppy with some neat ways?
And on and on and on and on
And on and on he went.
I'll never ask a zebra
About stripes
Again.

by Shel Silverstein

Tigers

I went to the zoo.
The tigers stride
backwards and forwards
safe inside:

Backwards and forwards...
Strong and stout
the great bars never
let them out,

But hour on hour
they're bound to go
backwards and forwards,
to and fro...

Their eyes are burning
yellow and brown.
They look like the sun
when the sun goes down.

Their muscles ripple
like a sea
under their skin.
They stared at me.

Strange, in a stranger's
land, they are,
with golden fingers
on the fur.

It is a topsy-
turvy thing
that men should catch
and cage a King.

by Jean Kenward

Algy

Algy met a bear,
A bear met Algy.
The bear was bulgy,
The bulge was Algy.

Anon

Tall Boy

Long neck tongue
Licking around the sun;
The tallest tree cannot escape
His measuring tape;
He stretches long
Lips smack into mouth-watering chew
Grips leaves in a sweet green stew.
Walking tall
He waits for the food-trees to call
His name in whispers:
'Giraffe' sounds like 'Get off!'

by Faustin Charles

Hippo Writes A Love Poem to his Wife

Oh my beautiful fat wife
Larger to me than life
Smile broader than the river Nile
My winsome waddlesome
You do me proud in the shallow of morning
You do me proud in the deep of night
Oh, my bodysome mud-basking companion.

by John Agard

The Hippopotamus

What fun	to be
A hippo	-potamus
And weigh	a ton
From top	to bottamus

by Michael Flanders

Hippo Writes
A Love Poem to
her Husband

Oh my lubby-dubby hubby-hippo
With your widely-winning lippo
My Sumo-thrasher of water
Dearer to me than any two-legger
How can I live without
Your ponderful potamus pout?

by John Agard

Rhinoceros

The ravenous rhino
Is big, strong and tough,
But his skin is all baggy and flappy,
Which means that there's plenty
Of room for his lunch,
And that makes him terrible happy.

by Giles Andreae

The Elephant

When people call this beast to mind,
They marvel more and more
At such a LITTLE tail behind,
So LARGE a trunk before.

by Hilaire Belloc

Index of First Lines

Picture credits

Cover image and title page:
NHPA (Daryl Balfour)

Bruce Coleman pp. 14 (Robert Maier),
18 (Adriano Bacchella),
27 (Pacific Stock); 31 (Mark N Boulton)
Images Colour Library p.6 (National
Geographic);
NHPA pp. 8 (Stephen Dalton), 12
(Hellion and Van Ingen), 30 (John Shaw);
Oxford Scientific Films pp. 4 (David
Dennis), 5 (Richard Packwood), 23
(Michael Pitts), 25 (David Tipling);
Robert Harding p.20 (Adam Woolfitt)
Still Pictures p.10 (Klein/Hubert).